American Politics Today

The U.S. Senate Today

John Ziff

ELDORADO INK

Eldorado Ink
PO Box 100097
Pittsburgh, PA 15233
www.eldoradoink.com

Produced by OTTN Publishing, Stockton, New Jersey

CPSIA compliance information: Batch#MAP2016.
For further information, contact Eldorado Ink at info@eldoradoink.com.

First printing

1 3 5 7 9 8 6 4 2

Library of Congress Cataloging-in-Publication Data

on file at the Library of Congress
    ISBN 978-1-61900-096-4 (hc)
    ISBN 978-1-61900-104-6 (pb)
    ISBN 978-1-61900-112-1 (trade)
    ISBN 978-1-61900-120-6 (ebook)

*For information about custom editions, special sales, or premiums,
please contact our special sales department at info@eldoradoink.com.*

Table of Contents

Chapter 1

"World's Greatest Deliberative Body"

Not a single senator questioned the nominee's professional qualifications. Not a single senator suggested he was unsuited for the position by character or temperament. Not a single senator voiced concerns about any incident from his 25-year career or pointed to troubling aspects of his private life. In short, John Bass—an experienced Foreign Service officer with a sterling reputation—was an uncontroversial choice to be U.S. ambassador to Turkey. And on September 17, 2014, the United States Senate—exercising its constitutional responsibility to provide "advice and consent" on high-level presidential appointments—confirmed Bass to that post. The vote was 98–0.

SHAMEFUL TACTIC?

Despite the unanimous confirmation vote, Bass's appointment hadn't proceeded smoothly. It had, in fact, been deliberately blocked in the

---

The U.S. Senate is made up of 100 senators—two from every U.S. state. Within the Senate there are 20 committees and 68 subcommittees, as well as four joint committees with the House of Representatives. The Senate meets in the U.S. Capitol Building in Washington, D.C.

Senate confirmation of John Bass, nominated to be ambassador to Turkey, and other officials was blocked by the Republican minority for six weeks during the summer of 2014. Bass eventually won unanimous confirmation and was sworn in to his new post in October 2014.

Senate for six weeks. And that delay had come at a most inopportune time. The previous ambassador to Turkey had retired, leaving the United States without a top-level diplomat in Ankara. Yet the United States was trying to secure Turkey's commitment to fight the Islamic State, an extremist group that was wreaking havoc in Iraq and Syria and that, many national security experts said, presented a serious threat to American interests. The absence of an ambassador could only hinder the difficult and delicate negotiations with the Turkish government.

"Blocking ambassadors when the world is in turmoil and America's national interest is at stake," noted Norman Ornstein, a congressional scholar at the conservative-leaning American Enterprise Institute, "is simply shameful."

Shameful or not, the treatment the Bass nomination received in the United States Senate was hardly surprising. In recent years, the upper chamber of Congress has proved increasingly unable to conduct even the most routine business expeditiously. Nasty partisanship has bred a state of affairs in which gridlock appears to be the norm.

The Senate has a mind-numbing body of procedural rules. But the institution really relies on "unanimous consent" to function. Under unanimous consent, a rule of procedure may be waived, as long as no senator objects. Unanimous consent streamlines the workings of the Senate, enabling routine proceedings to be handled quickly and efficiently.

Historically, the Senate has treated most ambassadorial nominations as routine business. Every nominee is vetted at a hearing before the Senate Committee on Foreign Relations. If the committee approves, the nomination is sent to the full Senate for a vote. Because most ambassadorial nominees are, like John Bass, career Foreign Service officers, the Senate has often confirmed a bloc of nominees with a single voice vote. This indicates an absence of controversy surrounding any of the nominees, the senators deeming it unnecessary to put their individual views on the record by means of roll-call votes.

On July 31, 2014, Senator Robert Menendez, a Democrat from New Jersey and chairman of the Foreign Relations Committee, requested unanimous consent for a voice vote to confirm 25 ambassadorial nominees. They included Bass, as well as others whose nominations had been pending for more than a year.

Senator Mike Enzi, a Republican from Wyoming, objected to the unanimous consent request. As a result, each nomination would have to be debated and voted on individually, following regular Senate order. With the Senate's five-week summer recess scheduled to begin August 1, Enzi's objection guaranteed that no action would be taken on the nominations until mid-September at the earliest.

Enzi voiced no substantive opposition to any of the nominees. Rather, he made clear that he was retaliating for Senate Democrats' decision to "take away some of the minority rights." He didn't use the

Under the rules of the Senate, individual senators can slow down discussions on legislation or presidential nominations, as Mike Enzi of Wyoming did in 2014.

term, but he was referring to the filibuster, a procedural tactic by which a minority of senators—just 41 of the Senate's 100 members—can stop a bill or a motion from proceeding to a floor vote by refusing to end debate.

GOING NUCLEAR

Use of the filibuster—once relatively rare—exploded during the 110th Congress (2007–2008) and 111th Congress (2009–2010). Democrats complained that after Barack Obama, a Democrat, became president in 2009, Republicans began using the filibuster in unacceptable ways. One such way, according to Democrats, was the wholesale blocking of presidential nominees.

When it comes to presidential appointments, deference to the chief executive's wishes—except under extraordinary circumstances—has historically been the norm. The president, it's understood, deserves wide latitude in assembling his or her governing team. So unless a cabinet secretary or undersecretary, an agency head, or other executive-branch nominee is tainted by scandal or is grossly unqualified, the Senate's strong inclination has been to confirm that nominee. The same holds true for judicial appointments below the Supreme Court. A 2014 report by the Congressional Research Service found that the Senate rejected less than 1 percent of U.S. circuit and district court nominees between 1939 and 2013. In large part, that's because of a long-standing consensus that presidents should be permitted to put their stamp on the federal judiciary. One of the prerogatives a president gains by winning election, according to this view, is the ability to fill judicial vacancies with judges who share the president's basic beliefs—provided they are professionally qualified, they face no allegations of malfeasance, and their judicial philosophy isn't deemed extreme.

Even controversial presidential nominees have usually been given an up-or-down vote in the Senate. Until recent times, filibustering nominees was an uncommon tactic.

Democrats, who held the majority in the Senate during the first six years of the Obama presidency, expressed outrage at what they viewed

Democrats complained that after the historic election of Barack Obama in November 2008, the Republican minority in the U.S. Senate misused the filibuster procedure to prevent Obama's nominees from taking office. Republicans noted that Democrats had employed the same tactics during the presidency of Obama's predecessor, George W. Bush.

as the Republican minority's obstructionism. "For the first time in the history of our republic," railed Harry Reid, the Senate majority leader, "Republicans have routinely used the filibuster to prevent President Obama from appointing an executive team and from appointing judges. The need for change is so, so very obvious." Reid threatened to pursue what had been dubbed the "nuclear option": changing the Senate's rules, by a simple-majority vote, to limit use of the filibuster.

Reid's Republican counterpart, Minority Leader Mitch McConnell, said that course of action would be nothing short of disastrous. It would, he claimed, "irreparably damage the Senate" and "contribute to the ruination of our country."

If McConnell sounded earnest, only a few years earlier he'd taken precisely the opposite position regarding the filibuster. So had Reid.

In 2005, Republican George W. Bush was beginning his second

term as president, and Republicans controlled the Senate. Democrats had filibustered 10 of Bush's judicial nominees. McConnell—who was then majority whip, the Republicans' number-two leader in the Senate—blasted the tactic as improper and threatened the nuclear option. "To correct this abuse," he said, "the majority in the Senate is prepared to restore the Senate's traditions and precedents to ensure that regardless of party, any President's judicial nominees, after full and fair debate, receive a simple up-or-down vote on the Senate floor. . . . The Constitution of the United States is at stake."

For his part, Reid—then the Senate minority leader—defended the filibuster as "an integral part of our country's 217 years of history." The filibuster, he said, "encourages moderation and consensus. It gives voice to the minority, so that cooler heads may prevail. . . . The filibuster serves as a check on power and preserves our limited government."

In the end, the "Gang of 14"—a group of seven Republican and seven Democratic senators—reached a deal that averted the nuclear option. The 2005 agreement provided for an end to the filibusters against some pending judicial nominees, and made no commitments regarding others. Gang of 14 members pledged not to filibuster future Bush nominees except under "extraordinary circumstances."

The defusing of the nuclear option proved short lived. Dozens of filibusters were mounted in 2009, and some Democratic senators began demanding reform. In 2011, Majority Leader Reid and Minority Leader McConnell struck a "gentleman's agreement" that helped forestall the nuclear option. Reid pledged to allow Republicans more opportunities to offer amendments to bills, while McConnell promised his party would cut back on its use of the filibuster.

But the agreement didn't hold. Republicans continued filibustering presidential nominees, and when they signaled that they would block anyone Obama tried to appoint to the influential U.S. Court of Appeals for the District of Columbia Circuit, Democrats had finally reached their limit.

Normally, 67 votes are needed to amend a Senate rule (except at the start of a new Congress). But on November 21, 2013, Reid used an unconventional parliamentary procedure to force a simple-majority vote on changing the filibuster. It passed, 52–48. Three Democratic senators joined all 45 Republicans in opposition.

The rules change essentially eliminated the filibuster for executive-branch nominees and nominees to circuit and district courts. Supreme Court nominees could still be filibustered, as could legislative motions.

If the actual changes to the filibuster were rather

Senator John McCain of Arizona was a leader of the "Gang of 14"—a group of senators from both parties who were willing to compromise to avoid a crisis over use of the filibuster.

modest, Republicans seethed—largely, they said, because Senate rules had been modified without a two-thirds majority. "It is nothing short of [a] complete and total power grab," Iowa's Charles Grassley charged. McConnell promised that the Democrats would come to regret their actions.

While the nuclear option enabled some long-stalled judicial nominations to proceed quickly to a confirmation vote, it didn't mean that all of President Obama's appointments were about to sail through the Senate. As of mid-July 2014, according to the nonpartisan group Common Cause, more than 120 presidential nominations were pending on the Senate floor. Even with a diminished ability to filibuster, Republicans retained a variety of tools for impeding the confirmation process. One was to refuse to vote on blocs of noncontroversial appointments, but rather to insist that nominees be considered individually, with up to 30 hours allotted for debate on each one. During the time set aside for debate, no other business can be conducted on the Senate floor—even when, as is often the case, no actual debate takes place.

Using this tactic, Republicans stopped more than 20 ambassador-ships from being filled before the Senate's 2014 summer recess. There were bitter recriminations from both sides of the aisle. Republicans said Democrats had only themselves to blame, for going through with the nuclear option. Democrats faulted Republicans for what they said was unprincipled obstructionism.

In the meantime, the United States had no ambassador in Turkey to help enlist that country's help in fighting the Islamic State. It had no ambassador in Vietnam, one of the countries U.S. officials hoped would back a maritime "code of conduct" to counter Chinese expansion in the strategic South China Sea. It had no ambassador in Guatemala, even as thousands of children fleeing that troubled Central American nation spawned a growing refugee crisis along the U.S. southern border. The Senate, it seemed, was incapable of rising above political partisanship and taking simple action to further the broader interests of the country.

Why did the United States Senate, long characterized as the "world's greatest deliberative body," become so dysfunctional? How did partisan rancor come to poison an institution once renowned for comity? Has gridlock become the norm in the upper chamber of Congress, or can an openness to compromise be restored? There are no simple answers to these questions.

Chapter 2

The Center Cannot Hold

In considering the polarization of today's Senate, it's important to bear in mind a couple points. First, bitter partisanship has characterized the Senate (and American political institutions overall) at other times in the nation's history. Second, the two major political parties have broad differences. They diverge not simply on specific policy questions, but on the proper role of government itself. Neither party is entirely consistent, of course, but in general the modern Republican Party advocates limited government, whereas the modern Democratic Party favors a more expansive use of federal authority. Given their basic philosophical differences, some friction between Democrats and Republicans in the Senate is inevitable.

That said, in past decades senators were less likely to conform rigidly to party ideology. For example, while the 1980 election of Ronald Reagan as president signaled conservatives' ascendancy in the Republican Party, the Senate Republican conference continued to include a number of socially moderate or even liberal members, many representing states in the Northeast or Midwest. Among the most prominent were Lowell Weicker of Connecticut, who served from 1971 to 1989; John Chafee of Rhode Island (1976–1999); Jack Danforth of Missouri (1976–1995); Nancy Kassebaum of Kansas (1978–1997);

John Warner of Virginia (1979–2009); and Arlen Specter of Pennsylvania (1981–2011). Similarly, while most Democrats in the Senate were socially and fiscally liberal, voters regularly sent a bloc of moderate-to-conservative Democrats to the upper chamber of Congress. Most came from southern states. They included Georgia's Sam Nunn (1972–1997); Alabama's Howell Heflin (1979–1997); John Breaux of Louisiana (1987–2005); Blanche Lincoln of Arkansas (1999–2011); and Evan Bayh of Indiana (1999–2011).

Liberals vs. Conservatives

When applied to the United States today, the terms *liberal* and *conservative* describe two opposing sets of political beliefs, as well as the people who hold them. Broadly speaking, liberals advocate a larger, more activist government than do conservatives.

Liberals generally favor significant government regulation of business, in order to achieve goals seen to be in the public interest (for example, environmental protection, the welfare of workers, consumer protection). Conservatives believe that the less the government intervenes in economic matters, the better. Free markets, conservatives say, produce the greatest benefits for society, including maximum prosperity.

Liberals believe government must fund "safety net" programs to ensure that all citizens have a minimum standard of living. Conservatives argue that government social spending tends to breed dependency and discourage work among the groups it's intended to help. Conservatives emphasize personal responsibility as the means by which the poor should improve their lives.

Compared with liberals, conservatives tend to be less open to cultural change and more desirous of preserving "traditional values." This dynamic can be seen, for example, in the issue of same-sex marriage.

In the United States, "left" or "left-wing" is synonymous with liberal. Conservatives are known as "right-wingers" or "the right."

The emergence of the Tea Party movement after 2009 has contributed to the polarization of the U.S. Senate.

Most observers agree that the presence of Democrats who were more conservative than their party as a whole, and of Republicans who were more liberal than theirs, helped the Senate function efficiently. These centrists often proved key to consensus building and compromise.

But Senate centrists have become an endangered species. That trend started receiving significant attention from the political media during the 2010 election cycle, when 10 Senate candidates (all of them Republicans) ran with backing from the conservative Tea Party movement. The Tea Party movement had burst into the spotlight in 2009. Its members were animated largely by what they deemed excessive federal spending and taxation. The movement channeled intense, even visceral, opposition to President Obama.

But Tea Party ire was hardly reserved for the president, or for Democrats. Tea Partiers also castigated moderate Republicans, whom they derisively referred to as RINOs ("Republicans in name only"). Many in the Tea Party disdained the very idea of political compromise. Polling conducted in September 2010 by the Pew Research Center found that 71 percent of people who identified with the Tea Party favored politicians who wouldn't compromise. That was substantially higher than the figure for people who identified with the Republican Party (59 percent) or the Democratic Party (40 percent).

In the end, the Tea Party's impact on Senate races in 2010 was mixed. Half of the candidates with Tea Party support—Ron Johnson (Wisconsin), Mike Lee (Utah), Rand Paul (Kentucky), Marco Rubio (Florida), and Pat Toomey (Pennsylvania)—won election. In Nevada, however, Republicans lost what appeared to be an excellent chance to oust Majority Leader Harry Reid—who suffered from abysmal approval ratings in his home state. Reid successfully tarred his Tea Party–backed opponent as an extremist—a view to which even a handful of prominent Nevada Republicans publicly subscribed.

In Delaware, Republican Mike Castle was considered a virtual shoo-in to win a special election for the seat formerly occupied by Joe Biden, who'd left the Senate to become vice president. Castle, a former governor and longtime congressman, was well known and popular. But he was also a moderate—and hence a target for Tea Party activists. They championed a conservative political novice, Christine O'Donnell, who scored a stunning upset over Castle in the Republican primary. O'Donnell's comically inept campaign enabled Democrat Chris Coons to breeze to victory in the general election.

For Senate Republicans, the lessons were hard to ignore. Departure from conservative orthodoxy could lead to a bruising primary challenge from highly energized Tea Partiers. Centrism was politically risky. Republicans who'd previously shown a willingness to compromise with Democrats began adopting more partisan stances.

But ideological polarization in the Senate was hardly confined to the Grand Old Party. In 2011, slightly more than half of all roll-call votes were "party unity" votes (in which a majority of GOP senators and a majority of Democratic senators come down on opposite sides). On average, 94 percent of Democrats stuck together on these party unity votes, according to Barbara Sinclair, a professor of political science at UCLA.

"An atmosphere of polarization and 'my way or the highway' ideologies has become pervasive in campaigns and in our governing institutions," lamented Olympia Snowe, a three-term Republican from Maine, in announcing that she wouldn't seek reelection in 2012. A casual observer might conclude that the situation Snowe described is of relatively recent origin. In fact, the trend toward ideological polarization in the Senate spans several decades.

Moderate Republicans like Olympia Snowe of Maine—those who tend to support the party on fiscal matters but have a more liberal voting record on social issues like abortion or gay rights—have largely disappeared from the U.S. Senate over the past two decades.

MEASURING POLARIZATION

Political scientists have developed various metrics for assessing the ideology of members of Congress. For example, the *National Journal* rates legislators on a liberal-conservative scale using a system created in 1981 by the political analyst Bill Schneider. Each year, roll-call votes deemed to reflect significant ideological distinctions are singled out. These votes are sorted into three issue categories—economic, social, and foreign policy. For each vote, the liberal and conservative position is identified. Each vote is also weighted, based on how closely the coalitions for and against the specific measure track with other votes in the same issue category. The assumption is that when distinct

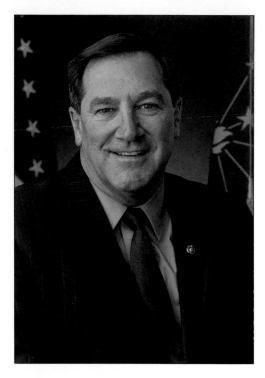

Senator Joe Donnelly of Indiana is one of the few conservative Democrats remaining in the U.S. Senate. While following the Democratic Party line on labor and economic issues, Donnelly often votes with Republicans on social issues and defense spending.

votes attract the same coalitions of legislators, those votes tend to be ideological in nature.

The percentage of times a given legislator casts a vote on the liberal or conservative side, and the weighted value of each vote, forms the basis of an index score in each of the three issue categories. Index scores allow senators (or representatives) to be compared with their colleagues ideologically on economic, social, and foreign policy issues. Every senator's voting record is ranked, from most liberal to most conservative, in each of those categories.

The three issue-based scores, in turn, are combined to generate a composite score that is supposed to reflect overall ideology. It's this metric that the *National Journal* uses to compile its annual vote ratings, with all 100 senators positioned on a most-liberal-to-most-conservative spectrum.

One might quibble (and critics often have) over certain aspects of the *National Journal* vote ratings. For example, the choice of which roll-call votes to include as good reflections of ideology can be somewhat subjective. A slightly different mix of votes might change an individual senator's ranking, which becomes particularly significant at either end of the spectrum. Democrats howled when the *National Journal*'s 2003 vote ratings—released in the midst of the 2004 presidential primary campaign—ranked John Kerry of Massachusetts, the Democratic front-runner and eventual nominee, as the most liberal member of the Senate. That distinction, a boon for Republicans who

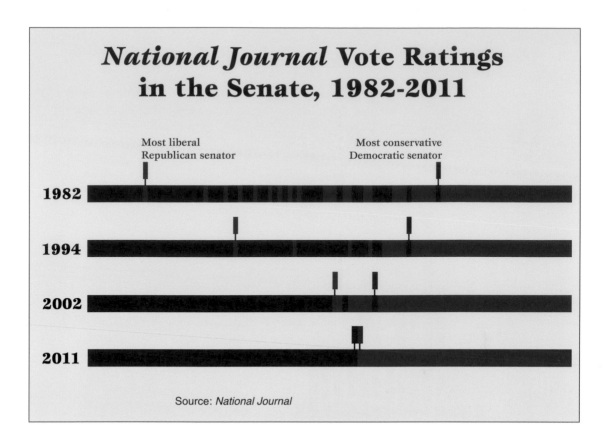

National Journal Vote Ratings in the Senate, 1982-2011

Most liberal
Republican senator

Most conservative
Democratic senator

1982

1994

2002

2011

Source: *National Journal*

wanted to paint Kerry as too liberal for the country, was based on just 25 votes Kerry had cast. The story was similar during the 2008 presidential race: the *National Journal* rated Barack Obama the most liberal member of the Senate in 2007. He'd ranked 11th most liberal the previous year.

If individual rankings can be second-guessed in any given year, the *National Journal*'s vote ratings do reveal trends over the longer term. In 1982, the first year the ratings were used, a solid majority of the Senate—58 members—compiled voting records that fell between those of the most liberal Republican and the most conservative Democrat. Eight years later, that number had shrunk to 34. By 2002, it stood at just 7. In 2010, there was no overlap at all: the most conservative Democrat had a voting record that was more liberal than the voting record of the most liberal Republican. The same held true for 2011, 2012, and 2013.

Polarization in the U.S. Senate

These charts show the ideological scores of U.S. Senators, based on roll-call votes and using the DW-NOMINATE methodology. Negative numbers represent liberal views; positive numbers, conservative views.

U.S. Senate, 93rd Congress (1973-74)

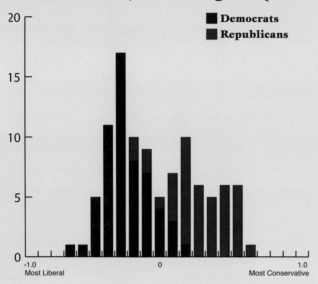

U.S. Senate, 112th Congress (2011-12)

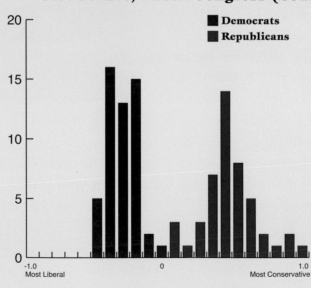

Sources: Voteview.com; Pew Research Center.

"There's a little bit of bumping around in the numbers here and there," noted Gary Jacobson, a professor of political science at the University of California–San Diego, "but the basic movement is toward the parties moving further and further apart."

That conclusion is supported by another widely used system for comparing legislators ideologically. Known as DW-NOMINATE, it was developed by two political science professors, Keith T. Poole of the University of California–San Diego and Howard Rosenthal of Princeton University.

DW-NOMINATE differs from the *National Journal* methodology in crucial ways. It doesn't involve selecting key votes that are judged to involve important ideological differences. Rather, DW-NOMINATE includes nearly all roll-call votes (unanimous votes are excluded), and it doesn't identify the supposed liberal or conservative position on any specific vote. DW-NOMINATE simply measures which legislators vote with which other legislators, and how often they do so. It's assumed that legislators who hold similar ideological views will vote with one another more often than they'll vote with legislators who hold dissimilar ideological views. It's further assumed that the most ideological legislators will join bipartisan voting coalitions the least frequently.

DW-NOMINATE's indirect way of measuring ideology yields results that track closely with results obtained through other methods, including the legislative "scorecards" compiled by interest groups such as the liberal Americans for Democratic Action and the American Conservative Union. And Poole and Rosenthal's system offers political scientists an extremely useful tool: a means of quantifying the ideological "distance" between the parties over time, on a scale that ranges from –1 (the liberal pole) to 1 (the conservative pole). Scores close to 0 represent centrist ideologies.

DW-NOMINATE broadly confirms the decades-long trend toward Senate polarization reflected in the *National Journal*'s annual vote rankings. Since the early 1980s, according to DW-NOMINATE scores, the average ideological positions of Democratic and Republican senators have steadily diverged. The Democratic caucus has become more liberal. The Republican conference has become more conservative, with the pace of the GOP's rightward move accelerating after 2005.

Poole and Rosenthal's methodology has been applied to Congresses all the way back to the beginning of the Republic. And the results indicate that the Senate in 2014 was more polarized than at any time since the Reconstruction era in the 1870s.

Polarization in contemporary American politics isn't unique to the upper chamber of Congress. In fact, DW-NOMINATE data show that the House of Representatives is significantly more polarized than the Senate.

In the House, however, the minority party has relatively few levers for derailing the agenda set by the majority party. That's not true in the Senate.

DELIBERATIVE BY DESIGN

The Founding Fathers viewed the Senate as a necessary check on the House of Representatives. The House, they feared, might be too responsive to the shifting desires of the public—or, as James Madison put it, might be inclined "to yield to the impulse of sudden and violent passions, and to be seduced . . . into intemperate and pernicious resolutions."

By design, the Senate was supposed to be more deliberative—and less democratic. The Constitution specified that senators be appointed by state legislatures rather than elected by the public (direct election of senators was mandated only with the ratification of the 17th Amendment in 1913). Moreover, Senate terms are for six years, whereas the members of the House serve for just two years at a time.

Beyond stating that each chamber of Congress "may determine the Rules of its Proceedings," the Constitution is largely silent about how the Senate or the House should operate. It's fair to say that the Senate's rules and procedures evolved in a way that more than fulfilled the Founding Fathers' wishes for a body resistant to hasty decision making.

Senate rules protect minority interests and perspectives from being ignored by the majority. Individual senators are guaranteed ample opportunity to have their voices heard, most notably through the right to debate at length and the right to offer amendments to bills at almost any time.

Senators enjoy other, informal prerogatives as well. For example, by tradition a single senator can delay a measure from reaching the floor of the Senate for consideration simply by notifying his or her floor leader (the Senate majority or minority leader). This practice is known as a "hold." Under another traditional prerogative, called the "blue slip," both senators from a judicial nominee's home state must give their consent before the nominee can even receive a hearing in the Judiciary Committee. A single senator can thus effectively veto a presidential nomination to the federal bench.

If there was one unifying rationale behind the development of the Senate's various rules, procedures, and traditions, it was this: that serious, thoughtful deliberation should be facilitated. Unlimited debate, for example, would allow a fulsome exchange of ideas, which could sharpen and clarify senators' thinking. The nearly unrestricted ability to offer amendments could correct problems in bills under consideration. A hold could give an individual senator time to study a complex issue before having to cast a vote.

But provisions designed to protect the rights of the minority can become cudgels against the majority. Provisions intended to elevate Senate deliberations can also be used to paralyze the institution.

The filibuster, an outgrowth of the Senate's tradition of unlimited debate, is the most obvious example. It wasn't until 1917 that Senate rules placed any restriction on the right of a senator to hold the floor indefinitely—a tactic that could be used not to persuade colleagues of the merits of a particular position, but merely to block voting on a measure. Under the 1917 rule change, the bar for ending filibusters was high: two-thirds of the senators present and voting had to vote for a motion to cut off debate, called cloture. If all members of the Senate were in attendance, and if none of them abstained from voting, 67 votes would be needed for cloture.

In 1975, under the direction of Majority Leader Mike Mansfield, a Democrat from Montana, the filibuster rules were changed again. The threshold for invoking cloture was lowered to three-fifths of the Senate—but that proportion referred to the number of sworn members of the body, not how many senators might be present and voting at a given time. So at least 60 votes would always be needed for cloture.

Mansfield also implemented a "two-track" system, which in effect allowed two pieces of business (one a filibustered measure) to be on the Senate floor at once. He thought this would make the Senate more efficient, by preventing all business from grinding to a halt during a filibuster. But there was an unintended consequence. To sustain a filibuster, senators previously had to hold the floor of the Senate by talking nonstop. That was grueling. The two-track system gave rise to what might be called the virtual filibuster, whereby a measure can be blocked (pending a successful cloture vote) simply by notifying the majority leader of the intent to filibuster. Mounting a filibuster no longer involved any effort or inconvenience for senators. And, because the process took place out of public view, little political risk attached to filibusters either. Mansfield's attempt to limit the effects of the filibuster had made it a more attractive weapon for minority obstruction.

Majority Leader Mike Mansfield (left) meets with Minority Leader Everett Dirksen, a Republican from Illinois, in 1967. Mansfield held the position of Senate Majority Leader from 1961 to 1977, longer than anyone in U.S. history. During his tenure he introduced changes that had the unintended effect of making filibusters more common.

A veritable arsenal of such weapons can be found in "Senate Procedure: Precedents and Practices." That document, the authoritative source for the Senate's parliamentary rules and procedures, runs to more than 1,600 pages.

NORMS OF RESTRAINT

During the 1980s and 1990s, control of the Senate swung from the Republicans to the Democrats and back again. The GOP held a majority in the Senate during the first six years of Republican Ronald Reagan's presidency (1981–1989). After winning control in 1987, the Democrats retained a Senate majority until 1995, a period that encompassed the entire presidency of Republican George H. W. Bush (1989–1993) and the first two years of Democrat Bill Clinton's administration (1993–2001). After that, Senate control remained in Republican hands for the duration of Clinton's presidency.

At no point during this two-decade span did either party hold 60 Senate seats. Thus, no filibuster supported by the entire minority party could be overcome. Ideological polarization was on the rise throughout the 1980s and 1990s, and there was a general trend toward the increased use of obstructive tactics such as the filibuster. Still, when they were in the minority neither Democrats nor Republicans deployed the full range of available procedural weapons to stifle the other party's agenda—or the agenda of the president.

Various factors, institutional and otherwise, help explain this fact. To begin, if the ideological center was shrinking steadily, it hadn't yet disappeared. Bipartisan coalitions could still be formed around most issues. Compromise wasn't denigrated; it was seen as essential.

Scholars also cite long-standing norms, or informal rules of behavior, that prevailed in the Senate. One important norm was reciprocity, which, note the political scientists Gregory J. Wawro and Eric Schickler, "entails that senators practice restraint in their exercise of their extensive individual prerogatives, including those that empower them to obstruct." A senator who did use his or her individual prerogatives to their fullest extent could expect to lose the cooperation of colleagues, who would use their individual prerogatives to block that senator at every turn.

Another important norm was "institutional patriotism," or loyalty to the Senate. "One who brings the Senate as an institution or senators as a class into disrepute," wrote the political scientist Donald R. Matthews in a seminal study of Senate folkways, "invites his own destruction as an effective legislator. . . . Senators are, as a group, fiercely protective of, and highly patriotic in regard to, the Senate." Excessive obstruction was seen as a form of disloyalty to the institution. It was understood that excessive obstruction could erode the Senate's legitimacy—something every senator was invested in protecting. "A loss of legitimacy," write Wawro and Schickler, "would have hurt individual senators, since it would have decreased the value of a Senate seat."

Personal friendships also played a powerful role in promoting cooperation, according to many longtime senators. Outside the Capitol, senators routinely socialized with colleagues from the other party. They formed deep friendships. "In those days," Joe Biden wrote of his early years in the Senate, "Democrats and Republicans actually enjoyed each other's company."

Deep ideological differences didn't preclude a close friendship, and the mutual trust and goodwill of friends could be the key to brokering a legislative compromise. Perhaps no pair epitomized this better than Ted Kennedy and Orrin Hatch. Kennedy, a Democrat from Massachusetts, was the Senate's best-known liberal. Hatch, a Republican from Utah, was a staunch conservative. "We fought each other like tooth and tongue," Hatch recalled, "but afterwards, we'd put our arms around each other and laugh about it. And we passed a lot of very important legislation together."

The Senate, which used to be a bastion of white men, has become more diverse in recent years. The 114th Congress, which began in 2015, featured a record 20 women serving in the Senate. There were just two African-American and three Hispanic senators, however.

One such piece of legislation was the Ryan White CARE Act. Passed in 1990, it provides assistance for Americans living with HIV/AIDS. Another important collaboration between Kennedy and Hatch was the State Children's Health Insurance Program (SCHIP), enacted in 1997. SCHIP covers millions of children who otherwise wouldn't have health insurance.

Other landmark legislation that originated in the Senate during the 1980s or 1990s included the Americans with Disabilities Act (ADA), introduced in 1988 by Iowa Democrat Tom Harkin. Two years later, the ADA passed the Senate on a voice vote and was signed into law by President Bush. Delaware's Joe Biden introduced the Violence Against Women Act (VAWA) in 1990. VAWA's path to enactment was circuitous. But in 1994, it finally passed Congress with bipartisan support, and President Clinton signed it into law.

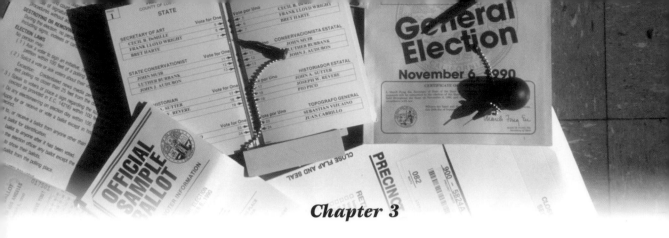

Chapter 3

Contentious Matters

Although senators did work together on some matters during the 1980s and 1990s, the Senate periodically witnessed bitter partisan fights. One such fight erupted in 1987, when President Reagan announced the nomination of a conservative judge, Robert Bork, to the Supreme Court. On July 1, within an hour of the White House announcement, Ted Kennedy delivered an inflammatory speech on the Senate floor:

> Robert Bork's America is a land in which women would be forced into back alley abortions, blacks would sit at segregated lunch counters, rogue police could break down citizens' doors in midnight raids, school children could not be taught about evolution, writers and artists could be censored at the whim of government, and the doors of the federal courts would be shut on the fingers of millions of citizens for whom the judiciary is—and is often the only—protector of individual rights that are the heart of our democracy.

Kennedy's speech presented a crude caricature of Bork's actual views, but the attack proved effective. Liberal advocacy groups quickly

Professor Anita Hill testifies before the Senate Judiciary Committee during a confirmation hearing for Clarence Thomas, a candidate for the U.S. Supreme Court, in October 1991.

Judge Robert Bork in September 1987, at the Senate hearing on his nomination to the Supreme Court.

launched a media campaign to portray Bork as an extremist, a narrative the Reagan administration struggled to counter. Ultimately, the Judiciary Committee sent Bork's nomination to the floor of the Senate with an unfavorable recommendation. On October 23, 1987, by a vote of 58–42, the full Senate rejected the nomination.

Republicans were infuriated, and many scholars suggest the episode had lasting effects. "The nomination," asserts Tom Goldstein, an attorney and cofounder of the award-winning legal-analysis website SCOTUSblog, "changed everything, maybe forever. . . . [The] fight legitimized scorched-earth ideological wars over nominations at the Supreme Court."

In 1991, another scorched-earth war raged in the Senate over a Supreme Court nominee. But ideology was only one ingredient in an explosive mix that also included race and sex. The conflict began after Associate Justice Thurgood Marshall—a giant of the civil rights movement and the only African American ever to have served on the Supreme Court to that point—announced his retirement. President George H. W. Bush nominated Clarence Thomas, a federal appeals court judge, to replace Marshall. Though African American, Thomas didn't share Marshall's liberal philosophy, and he was openly skeptical of affirmative action—the policy of actively seeking to promote educational or employment opportunities for members of groups that have suffered discrimination, such as African Americans and women.

In September, Thomas generated little controversy during five days of testimony before the Senate Judiciary Committee. But committee Democrats complained that he wasn't forthcoming in answering

Supreme Court nominee Clarence Thomas (left) testifies before the U.S. Senate Judiciary Committee in September 1991.

their questions, and several expressed doubts about his qualifications to serve on the nation's highest court. All six Republicans on the committee voted to endorse Thomas's nomination, and they were joined by one Democrat, Dennis DeConcini of Arizona, creating a 7–7 deadlock. The committee then voted to send the nomination to the full Senate without a recommendation.

Before the scheduled confirmation vote, however, a correspondent for National Public Radio broke a bombshell story: a former subordinate of Thomas's was accusing him of sexual harassment. She was Anita Hill, a law professor at the University of Oklahoma. Thomas had been Hill's boss at the Department of Education and at the Equal Employment Opportunity Commission.

On October 11, the Senate Judiciary Committee began three days of televised hearings to consider Hill's allegations. From the outset, the proceedings were acrimonious. Republicans and Democrats on the committee angrily sniped at each other. The tension was palpable.

Hill testified that Thomas had repeatedly pressured her to date him, which she'd always declined, and that he'd frequently brought up sexually explicit subjects during their interactions at work. Republican members of the Judiciary Committee subjected Hill to scathing questioning. Pennsylvania's Arlen Specter even accused her of perjury.

For his part, Thomas vehemently denied Hill's allegations. And, though his accuser was also African American, he leveled the incendiary charge that the proceedings were driven by racism. As far as he was concerned, Thomas said, the hearings were

> a high-tech lynching for uppity blacks who in any way deign to think for themselves, to do for themselves, to have different ideas, and it is a message that, unless you kow-tow to an old order, this is what will happen to you, you will be lynched, destroyed, caricatured by a committee of the U.S. Senate, rather than hung from a tree.

The Senate had rarely witnessed an uglier spectacle.

But the hearings didn't establish whether Hill or Thomas was telling the truth, and the Judiciary Committee again sent the nomination back to the full Senate without a recommendation. Ultimately, Thomas won confirmation by a slim 52–48 margin.

Anita Hill's treatment at the hands of the all-male Senate Judiciary Committee infuriated many women, with effects, Senate observers suggest, that carried over into the next elections. Ten women won Democratic or Republican primary races for Senate seats in 1992. Five, including incumbent Barbara Mikulski, triumphed in the general election, raising the Senate's female membership from just two to six.

From January to February 1999, another major political controversy had public attention riveted on the Senate. For only the second time in the nation's history, a president had been impeached. The previous December, the House of Representatives had approved two articles of impeachment against Bill Clinton—one for perjury, and the other for obstruction of justice. Both articles centered on a sexual relationship Clinton had with a White House intern named Monica Lewinsky.

Under the Constitution, it was the Senate's responsibility to decide whether to convict or acquit the president. Conviction would require a two-thirds majority and would result in the president's removal from office.

The first article of impeachment, charging that Clinton had provided false and misleading testimony to a grand jury about his relationship with Lewinsky, was defeated on a 45–55 vote. Ten Republicans joined all 45 Democrats in voting to acquit. By a 50–50 vote, the Senate rejected the second

This rally to protest the impeachment of President Bill Clinton was held in December 1998. The following February, the Senate acquitted the president.

article of impeachment, charging that Clinton had obstructed justice by encouraging Lewinsky to cover up their relationship. This time, five Republicans joined all the Democrats in voting to acquit.

In spite of the embarrassing revelations about his sexual indiscretions, Clinton came out of the impeachment saga with higher favorability ratings. While opinion polls showed that most Americans thought the charges against the president were true, most didn't think those charges were serious enough to remove him from office. In a *Los Angeles Times* poll conducted after the Senate trial, 65 percent of respondents said they approved of the outcome, while just 30 percent said Clinton should have been convicted. Still, a solid majority (57 percent) also disapproved of the way the Senate had handled the impeachment trial. Republicans, in particular, came in for harsh judgment. More than 60 percent of respondents said the GOP had pursued impeachment just to hurt Clinton politically. It remained to be seen whether voters would punish Republicans in the next elections.

CONTROVERSY, CALAMITY, AND CONSENSUS

The 2000 presidential election ranks among the most controversial political episodes in U.S. history. Nationwide, Democrat Al Gore received about a half million more votes than his Republican opponent, George W. Bush. But on election night, and even the following day, it wasn't clear which candidate would prevail in the Electoral College. The outcome hinged on Florida, where Bush was clinging to a razor-thin lead. An automatic machine recount completed three days after the election showed Bush the winner by 327 votes, out of close to 6 million cast. But lawyers for the Gore campaign requested manual recounts in four counties. Attorneys for the Bush campaign filed a federal lawsuit to halt all manual recounts. A tangle of litigation ensued.

On December 8, a full month after the election, the Florida Supreme Court ordered a manual recount of some 45,000 statewide "undervotes"—ballots that had been cast but for which voting machines had recorded no vote for president. Bush lawyers appealed the decision to the U.S. Supreme Court. On December 12, in a 5–4 decision in the case of *Bush v. Gore*, the Court ordered the recount stopped. Florida's 25 electoral votes went to George W. Bush, making him president.

In a concession speech, Gore urged the country to put aside the partisan rancor the election had engendered. Yet many of his supporters remained bitter. Many thought the Supreme Court's conservative justices had decided *Bush v. Gore* not on the legal merits but because of their own partisan preferences. Some legal scholars agreed. Among them was Harvard Law professor Alan Dershowitz, who called *Bush v. Gore* "the single most corrupt decision in Supreme Court history." Nearly one-quarter of Americans, according to a Gallup poll conducted in January 2001, believed Bush had stolen the election, and an additional 31 percent believed he'd won only on a technicality. Among the 45 percent who thought Bush had won the election "fair and square," most were Republicans.

The controversy surrounding the presidential election obscured an extraordinary result stemming from the 2000 Senate races: for the

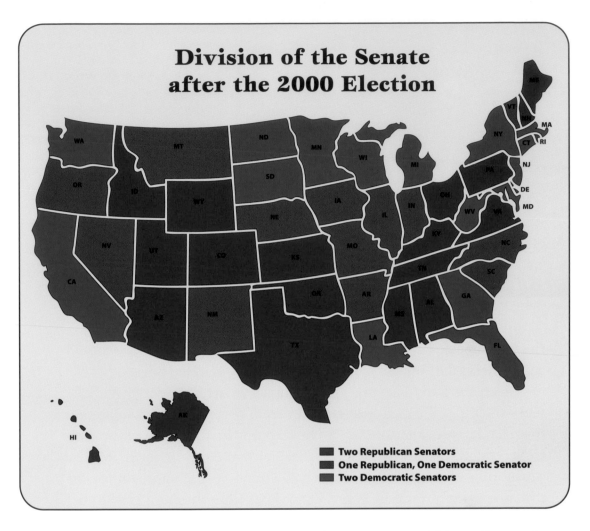

Division of the Senate after the 2000 Election

Two Republican Senators
One Republican, One Democratic Senator
Two Democratic Senators

first time ever, the upper chamber of Congress would be split evenly between 50 Republicans and 50 Democrats. Under the Constitution, the vice president is president of the Senate. In the event a Senate vote is tied, the vice president may cast the deciding vote.

For 17 days beginning January 3, 2001, when the new Senate was sworn in, Vice President Gore gave Democrats an effective majority by virtue of his tie-breaking authority. On January 20, when Dick Cheney was sworn in as vice president of the United States, control of the Senate shifted to the Republicans.

The Republicans didn't remain in control long, however. On May 24, Senator James Jeffords of Vermont announced that he was leaving

Senators Christopher Dodd, a Democrat from Connecticut, and Jim Jeffords, a moderate Republican from Vermont, speak at a 2000 event on child care for military families. The two men had worked together on the Senate Health, Education, Labor and Pensions Committee. According to later reports, in the spring of 2001 Dodd encouraged Jeffords to leave the Republican Party and become an Independent. Jeffords's decision to make this switch in May 2001 marked the first time that control of the Senate had changed parties without an election.

the Republican Party to become an Independent and that he would caucus with the Democrats.

Given the hotly disputed circumstances by which George W. Bush had gained the White House, it might seem reasonable to assume that his agenda would encounter a choke point in the Democratic-controlled (albeit closely divided) Senate. But that didn't happen. Within six months of taking office, Bush had gotten Senate approval for his top domestic priorities. The Economic Growth and Tax Relief Reconciliation Act, providing for large tax cuts, passed the Senate by a margin of 58–33 (with 9 senators not voting) on May 23. On June 14, by a vote of 91–8, the Senate passed the No Child Left Behind Act, which embodied the president's signature education-reform initiative.

This didn't necessarily signal a reversal of the trends toward increased partisanship and obstruction in the Senate. New presidents often enjoy a "honeymoon period," during which the opposition party tends to give them some deference and their own party tends to be uncommonly united. Such honeymoon periods, presidential historians note, don't generally extend beyond the summer of the president's first year.

Whatever trajectory Bush's relations with Congress may have

taken, everything changed with the al-Qaeda terrorist attacks of September 11, 2011. In the aftermath of those attacks, Congress united firmly behind the president, whose public approval spiked.

On September 14, Congress issued a joint resolution (it passed the Senate in a voice vote) authorizing the president to "use all necessary and appropriate force against those nations, organizations, or persons he determines planned, authorized, committed, or aided the terrorist attacks that occurred on September 11, 2001, or harbored such organizations or persons." The following month, American forces attacked

Congress set aside partisan differences in the wake of the September 11 terrorist attacks, passing homeland security legislation intended to protect U.S. citizens from further attacks.

Afghanistan, which was harboring al-Qaeda leader Osama bin Laden and many of the organization's fighters.

More major legislation grew out of the September 11 attacks. The Senate passed the USA PATRIOT Act, by a vote of 98–1, on October 24. President Bush signed it into law the next day. Among other provisions, the PATRIOT Act gave the government significantly broader surveillance authority in the name of combating terrorism.

In 2002, the Bush administration pushed hard for a congressional authorization to use military force against Iraq. The administration offered multiple rationales for why such authorization was needed. Chief among them were the claims that the Iraqi government had links to al-Qaeda, and that Iraq possessed so-called weapons of mass destruction (nuclear, chemical, or biological weapons), in violation of United Nations resolutions ordering it to disarm after the 1991 Gulf

American soldiers on patrol in Fallujah, Iraq. Most members of the Senate approved the Bush administration's request to send troops to Iraq in 2002. However, many Democrats came to regret their vote when it became clear that the president's case for war had been based on inaccurate information. The last American troops did not leave Iraq until 2011.

War. A congressional authorization to use military force, President Bush argued, would pressure Iraqi dictator Saddam Hussein to fulfill his country's disarmament obligations. On October 11, 2002, a day after the House of Representatives had done so, the Senate approved the Authorization for Use of Military Force Against Iraq Resolution. The vote was 77–23, with 29 Democrats joining all but one Republican in support of the measure.

Five weeks later, the Homeland Security Act passed the Senate with even broader support. Ninety senators voted for the act, which created the Department of Homeland Security (DHS) and required a major reorganization of the federal government to bring various agencies under its purview. DHS was supposed to make the country safer from terrorist attack.

FAULT LINES

Notwithstanding the bipartisan consensus on antiterrorism measures, relations between Senate Democrats and Republicans—and between Senate Democrats and the president—had begun to fray. In fact, during the 107th Congress—Bush's first two years in office—the number of cloture votes in the Senate ticked up to 61, an all-time high. The old record of 58 had been established during the 106th Congress.

Republicans held a slim 51–49 majority in the 108th Congress. While cloture votes declined significantly, Republicans seethed over Democrats' filibustering of 10 of President Bush's appellate court nominees, all of whom would have won confirmation in a straight up-or-down vote. It was, the Republicans charged, an unprecedented tactic—and that charge was largely true. Before George W. Bush became president, judicial nominations had been filibustered only in a few isolated instances, when there was some extraordinary concern or circumstance. Now, Democrats were applying a new standard: if all the Democrats on the Judiciary Committee voted against any nominee, then the Democratic caucus would do everything it could to stop that nominee, including use of the filibuster.

On the other hand, Republicans had also stopped significant numbers of Clinton judicial nominees from getting an up-or-down vote.

They hadn't used the filibuster—but they hadn't needed to, since they were in the majority and hence controlled the Judiciary Committee. "We Republicans are not blameless here," admitted Senator John McCain of Arizona. "For all intents and purposes, we filibustered Clinton's judges, by not letting them out of committee."

Senate norms were clearly eroding. That was underscored by Majority Leader Bill Frist in dramatic, if symbolic, fashion during the 2004 campaign. Frist traveled to South Dakota, the home state of Minority Leader Tom Daschle, to campaign against Daschle's reelection. Never before had any Senate leader campaigned openly against his counterpart. Frist was unapologetic, saying he merely wanted to expand his party's majority in the Senate. "One vote matters," the Tennessee Republican said. "Policy matters. Elections matter."

That explanation didn't satisfy Robert Byrd, who'd been serving in the Senate since 1959. "It used to be unheard of for Senate leaders to seek an active role against each other in campaigns," the West Virginia Democrat lamented. "That time has apparently gone. Has honor gone, too? Who cares about honor when a Senate seat might be gained?"

Ultimately, Daschle was defeated in a close race, and the Republicans recorded a net gain of four Senate seats in the 2004 elections. The GOP would enjoy a solid 55–45 majority in the 109th Congress.

In 2005, the bipartisan Gang of 14 resolved the stand-off over the Democrats' blocking of Bush's judicial nominees. Increasingly, though, one divisive matter came to dominate the Senate's attention. "I feel like every morning, I wake up, get a concrete block and have to walk around with it all day," complained Republican Jim DeMint of South Carolina. "We can't even address the issues." The "concrete block" to which DeMint referred was the war in Iraq.

Amid assurances that the fighting would be over quickly, the Bush administration had launched an invasion of Iraq and toppled Saddam Hussein in March 2003. But the occupation had turned into a bloody quagmire. In addition, no weapons of mass destruction had been found in Iraq. Serious questions emerged about whether the adminis-

During the 2004 election, Majority Leader Bill Frist (left) actively campaigned against Minority Leader Tom Daschle (right)—a sign, many observers felt, that the Senate's traditional spirit of cooperation among colleagues had been lost.

tration had misused intelligence in order to justify the invasion in the first place.

In 2006, Senate Democrats offered multiple proposals for the withdrawal of U.S. forces from Iraq. They ranged from a nonbinding resolution urging a pullout, to a plan that would make the president submit a timetable for a phased withdrawal, to an amendment that would impose a firm deadline for U.S. troops to be out of Iraq. None of the measures gained traction. Republicans accused Democrats of favoring a "cut and run" strategy, and Democrats were divided.

Iraq was a major issue in the 2006 midterm elections, however, and Democrats benefited. The GOP lost control of both chambers of Congress, with the Democratic Party gaining a substantial majority in the House of Representatives and a thin, 51–49 advantage in the Senate. (The Democrats' Senate majority included two Independents.) In the wake of the elections, President Bush pledged to work with the new Democratic-controlled Congress. Harry Reid, the incoming Senate majority leader, called for bipartisanship.

Chapter 4

Paralysis and Partisanship

Bipartisanship didn't suddenly break out in the Senate in 2007. In fact, the year marked a watershed in the institution's descent to routinized gridlock. More cloture votes took place in 2007 alone than had occurred in any previous two-year Congress. Many of the Republican filibusters were aimed at measures involving the Iraq War. But even some legislation that normally wouldn't arouse any partisan disagreement—such as an omnibus farm bill—was filibustered.

House Democrats simmered. Time and again, they watched bills they'd passed languish in the Senate for want of the 60 votes needed to invoke cloture. "You may call it the Democratic [Senate] majority, as I once did," observed Representative Charlie Rangel, a New York Democrat, "but they're being held hostage by the Republican minority."

For their part, Senate Republicans pointed a finger at the majority. Increased use of the filibuster, they said, was necessary because

Tourists visit the Capitol Building in Washington, D.C. U.S. senators are considerably wealthier than the people they represent. In 2013, according to the Center for Responsive Politics, the median net worth of a U.S. Senator was $2.8 million. The median net worth of all American households was $56,355.

Democrats were pursuing a politicized agenda and were loath to compromise. "I think we can stipulate once again for the umpteenth time," Minority Leader Mitch McConnell said, "that matters that have any level of controversy about it in the Senate will require 60 votes."

In any event, the Senate held 112 cloture votes during the 110th Congress. That mark shattered the previous record of 61.

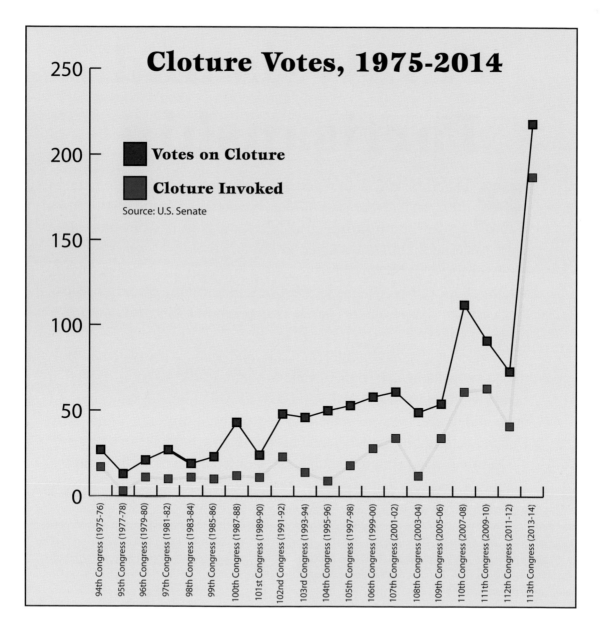

The 2008 elections saw a Democrat, Barack Obama, win the White House and the Democratic Party increase its majorities in both chambers of Congress. As of January 2009, the Democrats held a 58–41 edge in the Senate. The outcome of one extremely tight race—between Republican Norm Coleman and Democrat Al Franken in Minnesota—had yet to be determined, pending the outcome of a legal challenge.

With the U.S. economy mired in the biggest downturn since the 1930s, Congress in February 2009 passed the American Recovery and Reinvestment Act (ARRA). A package of government spending increases and tax cuts, ARRA was intended to stimulate the foundering economy. But many Republicans objected to the price tag, approximately $800 billion, amid a steadily rising national debt. In the Senate, only three Republicans—Maine's Susan Collins and Olympia Snowe, and Pennsylvania's Arlen Specter—joined the Democratic caucus in voting for the bill.

In April, Specter bolted the GOP and joined the Democratic Party. That defection—combined with the swearing-in of Minnesota's Al Franken in July, after the courts had certified him the winner of the contested Senate race—gave the Democrats 60 seats. If they maintained complete party unity, they could defeat any filibuster.

Health care reform was on the legislative agenda—and very much

Senator Arlen Specter of Pennsylvania discusses the American Recovery and Reinvestment Act in Philadelphia, February 2009. Two months later, the Republican would switch parties. "As the Republican Party has moved farther and farther to the right, I have found myself increasingly at odds with the Republican philosophy and more in line with the philosophy of the Democratic Party," Specter explained. Critics noted that Specter had been unlikely to win the Republican Party's nomination in the 2010 primary.

in the public spotlight—during the summer of 2009. Creating a system of universal health insurance had been a major Obama campaign promise, and the Democrats took up the issue early in the 111th Congress. In the House of Representatives, three committees held hearings throughout the spring, ultimately collaborating on a bill that was introduced in mid-July. It had no GOP support and, Republicans charged, had been crafted without any substantive input from them.

The Senate took a different approach. Responsibility for writing a health care bill fell to the Finance Committee, and its chairman, Max Baucus of Montana, was eager to create a bipartisan product. Baucus set up an informal group of committee members—the so-called Gang of Six—to negotiate a legislative framework that would garner support from both parties. In addition to Baucus, the Gang of Six included fellow Democrats Kent Conrad of North Dakota and Jeff Bingaman of New Mexico. The Republican members were Olympia Snowe, Wyoming's Mike Enzi, and Iowa's Charles Grassley.

The group spanned the ideological spectrum, from the reliably liberal Bingaman to the solidly conservative Enzi. Moderates Conrad and Snowe both enjoyed reputations as consensus-seekers. But Baucus believed Grassley, his close friend and the Finance Committee's ranking member (the senior member from the minority party), would be the key to getting a substantial number of Republicans to sign on to health care reform. In 1993, Grassley—along with GOP Senate colleagues John Chafee, Orrin Hatch, and David Durenberger—had written and introduced the Health Equity and Access Reform Today Act. The bill was the main Republican alternative to the health reform legislation backed by the Clinton administration, and Baucus made it the starting point for the Gang of Six negotiations.

By the beginning of summer, several months into their talks, the group appeared to be making progress toward a bipartisan agreement. And polls showed that most Americans wanted something done about the nation's health care system. A *USA Today*/Gallup survey conducted July 10–12, for example, showed 56 percent in favor of Congress passing major health care reform legislation in 2009, and 33 percent opposed.

President Barack Obama and Vice President Joe Biden discuss health care reform with four key senators in 2009: (from left) Senate Finance Committee chairman Max Baucus (D-Montana); Michael Enzi (R-Wyoming), the ranking member of the Senate Committee on Health, Education, Labor and Pensions; Charles Grassley (R-Iowa), the ranking member of the Senate Finance Committee; and Chris Dodd (D-Connecticut), the senior member of the Senate Committee on Health, Education, Labor and Pensions.

In a few short weeks, however, public opinion shifted dramatically. A Gallup poll conducted August 6–9 found that people were about evenly divided over whether they wanted their representatives to vote for a health care bill (35 percent in favor, 36 percent opposed). The intensity of the opposition, though, was striking—as many senators discovered during their summer recess, when constituents angrily confronted them at town hall meetings and other events. Provisions in, or said to be in, the House bill led many Americans to fear a coming "government takeover" of health care, with federal bureaucrats rather than doctors deciding which treatments patients could receive—and even deciding when an elderly or chronically ill patient should stop receiving treatment altogether.

By the time Congress returned from its summer recess in September, it was clear that Baucus's dream of crafting a bipartisan health care bill had been extinguished. Among the GOP members of the Gang of Six, only Snowe remained engaged in the negotiations. Enzi made plain that he wouldn't back any bill. Grassley told a reporter that he wouldn't vote for any bill that didn't enjoy broad-based Republican support—which essentially amounted to the same thing, as the Senate GOP conference was firmly opposed to the legislation taking shape in the Finance Committee. Minority Whip Jon Kyl of Arizona said that to get Republican support, the Democrats would have to start negotiations from scratch.

Instead, in mid-October, the Finance Committee voted out a bill. Snowe was the lone Republican to join all the Democrats in approving the measure.

A heated, and at times shrill, public debate raged throughout the fall of 2009. A few Democratic senators wavered in their support of health care reform. To ensure the backing of these senators, the White House and Democratic leadership in the Senate cut deals with them. None was more controversial than the so-called Cornhusker kickback, a deal to guarantee the support of Senator Ben Nelson of Nebraska, by which U.S. taxpayers would pay $100 million to expand Medicaid (a publicly funded health care program for the poor) in Nelson's home state.

In December, Democrats overcame a Republican filibuster and passed, on a strict party-line vote, the Patient Protection and Affordable Care Act. It included the requirement that every American have health insurance or be subject to a tax penalty; provided for state-based "exchanges" where people could buy their insurance; and subsidized the cost for those with more modest incomes. In these respects, the Senate bill resembled the legislation passed in the House of Representatives in November. But unlike the House version, the Senate bill didn't contain a "public option"—a federally run insurance program that would compete with private insurance companies.

The Senate and House would have to resolve their differences in a conference committee. Then both chambers would vote (without the

President Barack Obama signs an executive order related to the Patient Protection and Affordable Care Act, March 2010. The decision by Democrats to use the reconciliation process to pass the health care legislation in the Senate angered many Republicans.

ability to offer amendments) on the resulting bill, called a conference report.

Before that happened, however, Democrats were dealt a major blow. On January 19, 2010, Republican Scott Brown won a special election in Massachusetts to serve out the remainder of Ted Kennedy's Senate term (Kennedy had died the previous August). Now Democrats no longer had 60 votes to break a Republican filibuster.

Unless the House voted for the Senate bill, health care reform was dead. But many House Democrats objected to provisions in the Senate legislation. To win them over, President Obama and Speaker of the House Nancy Pelosi promised to address their concerns in another bill, which could be passed in the Senate through a controversial procedure known as reconciliation.

Republicans expressed outrage, and even some Democrats quietly said they were uneasy with the tactic. Reconciliation bills—which must involve budget-related matters—can't be filibustered, and the ability to offer amendments is limited. All 41 Senate Republicans signed a letter saying it was inappropriate for the Democrats to use reconciliation "to pass a partisan bill that is opposed by the majority of Americans." Gallup polling conducted in early March 2010 did, in fact, show that by a small margin (48 percent to 45 percent) Americans were opposed to the Democratic health care plan.

Nonetheless, on March 21, 2010, the House narrowly approved the Patient Protection and Affordable Care Act, then effectively amended the bill by passing the Health Care and Education Reconciliation Act. After President Obama signed the former act into law, the Senate took up and passed the latter, with a couple amendments, on March 25. The vote was 56–43, with three Democrats joining all 40 Republicans who were present in voting against the bill.

Chapter 5

A Broken Institution

After the enactment of the Affordable Care Act, Mitch McConnell excoriated the Democrats for what he characterized as a "power grab," saying that the use of reconciliation to pass health care legislation represented "the culmination of a year-long quest by a partisan majority to force its will on the public."

At the very least, that characterization failed to present the whole story. Democrats did ultimately resort to a controversial parliamentary procedure to prevail, but they hadn't set out to "force their will" on the public—or on the Republican minority. If they had, the Senate Finance Committee would have voted out a bill in June or July of 2009, and with a filibuster-proof 60 seats, Democrats would have quickly pushed it through the full Senate.

Democrats wanted GOP colleagues to sign on to a health care reform bill, and they were willing to make policy concessions in order to bring that about. But Republicans passed up the opportunity to help shape the legislation. They did so for strategic reasons, as Mitch McConnell confessed in a candid moment. "It was absolutely critical that everybody be together," McConnell said, "because if the proponents of the bill were able to say it was bipartisan, it tended to convey to the public that this is O.K., they must have figured it out."

McConnell's strategy of denying Democrats the mantle of bipartisanship was evident with other legislation, including the Bipartisan Task Force for Responsible Fiscal Action Act. Coauthored by Kent Conrad and New Hampshire's Judd Gregg—the Senate Budget Committee's chairman and ranking member, respectively—the act was expressly designed to reduce the federal deficit, a major stated priority of the Republican Party. The act would set up an 18-member bipartisan group whose recommendations for deficit reduction would be fast-tracked to the floor of the Senate and House of Representatives.

McConnell repeatedly expressed his support for the measure. "We must address the issue of entitlement spending now before it is too late," he declared in a 2009 floor speech. "As I have said many times before, the best way to address the crisis is the Conrad-Gregg proposal." McConnell continually hammered President Obama for failing to support the measure, which some liberal economists believed was ill advised while the country's economy remained sluggish. Still, the act eventually garnered 34 cosponsors, including 15 members of the Democratic caucus.

In early 2010, Obama came out in support of the Conrad-Gregg proposal, which was scheduled for a vote. Seven Republican cosponsors abruptly withdrew their support. McConnell joined them, along with 38 others, in a filibuster that succeeded in quashing the bill. "Never before have cosponsors of a major bill conspired to kill their own idea, in an almost Alice-in-Wonderland fashion," noted congressional scholars Thomas Mann and Norman Ornstein. "Why did they do so? Because President Barack Obama was for it, and its passage might gain him political credit."

It would be difficult to imagine a starker illustration of how broken the Senate had become. After decades of gradually escalating partisanship, after decades of rising levels of obstruction—from Republicans and Democrats alike—the institution's norms of restraint had been shattered. Cooperation and consensus-seeking had given way to a state of perpetual conflict. A tooth-and-nail fight was liable to break out even when both sides agreed on the policy in question.

Procedural battles raged incessantly during the 112th and 113th Congresses, when Democrats enjoyed majorities of a 53–47 and 55–45, respectively. The Republican minority engaged in a seemingly endless series of delaying actions, making a 60-vote supermajority the requirement to conduct virtually any Senate business, significant or mundane. The 113th Congress witnessed a staggering 218 cloture votes.

A strong GOP showing in the 2014 elections brought the Republicans control of the Senate and made Mitch McConnell majority leader.

On the other hand, Majority Leader Harry Reid made unprecedented use of a parliamentary tactic known as "filling the amendment tree" to deny Republicans any chance to offer amendments to legislation. The tactic relies on the prerogative of the majority leader to have his amendments considered before those of other senators. By offering multiple trivial amendments, the majority leader can use up the allotted 30 hours of debate time after a cloture vote. Of the more than 50 bills that received roll-call votes in the Senate during the 113th Congress, just 4 had more than five votes on amendments, according to the Government Affairs Institute at Georgetown University.

The GOP won big in the 2014 midterm elections, netting nine seats in the Senate. Mitch McConnell was thus able to realize his lifelong dream of becoming majority leader. McConnell pledged to fix a Senate he acknowledged was broken and hadn't been getting anything done. "This gridlock and dysfunction," he said, "can be ended."

McConnell promised to make the Senate more productive by restoring "regular order"—the rules, precedents, and customs by which the institution had historically conducted its business—which he accused his predecessor of ignoring. Among the commitments he made in this vein was to allow full debate and to permit members of

President Obama and Vice President Biden meet with bicameral leadership of Congress in the Oval Office. Seated on the left are the Republicans, Speaker of the House John Boehner (Ohio) and Senate Majority Leader Mitch McConnell (Kentucky). On the right are the Democrats, Senate Minority Leader Harry Reid (Nevada) and House Minority Leader Nancy Pelosi (California).

both parties to offer extensive amendments to legislation. The notion that such gestures might win the goodwill of Democrats seems odd, given the relentlessly obstructive approach McConnell had adopted when Republicans were in the minority. Less than a month into his new job, McConnell would learn just how disinclined the new minority was to forgive and forget.

On January 12, 2015, the Senate took up a bill to approve the Keystone XL oil pipeline. Over the next couple weeks, dozens of amendments to the bill were offered, by Republicans and Democrats alike. GOP leaders noted proudly that the Senate voted on more amendments to the Keystone XL bill alone than Harry Reid had allowed for all legislation reaching the Senate floor the previous year. But, after cloture on the Keystone bill had been attempted and failed, McConnell blocked Democrats from explaining or debating their amendments, even briefly. Democrats pounced, berating and mocking McConnell for so quickly breaking his promise to return the Senate to regular order.

In March, howls of protest erupted from McConnell's own conference after the majority leader filled the amendment tree to prevent conservative Republicans from offering amendments to foul a bill funding the Department of Homeland Security. The conservatives wanted to use a potential DHS shutdown to pressure President Obama to rescind an executive order on immigration.

By the time Congress went on its summer recess in August 2015, McConnell had filled the amendment tree—a tactic for which he'd lambasted Harry Reid mercilessly—a half-dozen times. Perhaps that shouldn't have surprised anyone. The ideals to which the "world's greatest deliberative body" once aspired—unflagging respect for colleagues, cooperation, institutional patriotism, the quest for consensus solutions to the nation's problems—are incompatible with the hyperpartisan nature of contemporary American politics. "It's kind of hard to get back to a Senate where the Senate works in that type of a fluid, collegial place," observes George Washington University political science professor Sarah Binder. "Because that's just not the world—partisan or ideological—that we live in."

Chapter Notes

p. 6: "Blocking ambassadors . . ." Laura Hancock, "Heat Follows Enzi for Delaying, Blocking Ambassador Votes," *Billings Gazette*, April 1, 2014. http://billingsgazette.com/news/state-and-regional/wyoming/heat-follows-enzi-for-delaying-blocking-ambassador-votes/article_04072b22-c970-5e9f-b910-7ef74760c755.html

p. 7: "take away some . . ." *Congressional Record*, vol. 160, no. 122 (July 31, 2014): S5212. http://www.gpo.gov/fdsys/pkg/CREC-2014-07-31/html/CREC-2014-07-31-pt1-PgS5211-2.htm

p. 9: "For the first time . . ." Tom McCarthy, "Senate Approves Change to Filibuster Rule After Repeated Republican Blocks," *The Guardian*, November 21, 2013. http://www.theguardian.com/world/2013/nov/21/harry-reid-senate-rules-republican-filibusters-nominations

p. 9: "irreparably damage . . ." Isaac Chotiner, "GOP: Ending Filibusters Is Unconstitutional and Un-American—and We'll Do It, Too," *New Republic*, November 22, 2013. http://www.newrepublic.com/article/115711/filibuster-reform-gop-hates-nuclear-option-threatens-worse

p. 10: "To correct this abuse . . ." *Congressional Record—Senate*, vol. 151, no. 67 (May 19, 2005): S5470. http://www.gpo.gov/fdsys/pkg/CREC-2005-05-19/pdf/CREC-2005-05-19-pt1-PgS5453-5.pdf

p. 10: "an integral part . . ." "Reid Floor Speech on Use of Filibuster," May 18, 2005. United States Senate Democrats. http://democrats.senate.gov/2005/05/18/reid-floor-speech-on-use-of-filibuster/

p. 10: "encourages moderation . . ." Ibid.

p. 11: "It is nothing short . . ." McCarthy, "Senate Approves Change to Filibuster Rule."

p. 18: "An atmosphere of polarization . . ." Amy Davidson, "Why Olympia Snowe Won't Run," *The New Yorker*, February 28, 2012. http://www.newyorker.com/news/amy-davidson/why-olympia-snowe-wont-run

p. 20: "There's a little bit . . ." Ronald Brownstein, "Pulling Apart," *National Journal*, February 24, 2011. http://www.nationaljournal.com/magazine/congress-hits-new-peak-in-polarization-20110224

p. 22: "to yield to the impulse . . ." [James Madison], *The Federalist* No. 62. http://www.constitution.org/fed/federa62.htm

p. 22: "may determine the Rules . . ." Constitution of the United States. http://www.archives.gov/exhibits/charters/constitution_transcript.html

p. 25: "entails that senators . . ." Gregory J. Wawro and Eric Schickler, *Filibuster: Obstruction and Lawmaking in the U.S. Senate* (Princeton, NJ: Princeton University Press, 2013), p. 43.

p. 26: "One who brings the Senate . . ." Ibid.

p. 26: "A loss of legitimacy . . ." Ibid.

p. 26: "In those days . . ." Joe Biden, *Promises to Keep: On Life and Politics* (New York: Random House, 2008), p. 89.

p. 26: "We fought each other . . ." "Sen. Hatch Remembers His Friend Ted Kennedy," *All Things Considered*, National Public Radio, August 26, 2009. http://www.npr.org/templates/story/story.php?storyId = 112264375

p. 29: "Robert Bork's America . . ." Norman Vieira and Leonard Gross, *Supreme Court Appointments: Judge Bork and the Politicization of Senate Confirmations* (Carbondale: Southern Illinois University Press, 1998), p. 26.

p. 30: "The nomination changed everything . . ." Nina Totenberg, "Robert Bork's Supreme Court Nomination 'Changed Everything, Maybe Forever,'" *All Things Considered*, National Public Radio, December 19, 2012. http://www.npr.org/sections/itsallpolitics/2012/12/19/167645600/robert-borks-supreme-court-nomination-changed-everything-maybe-forever

p. 32: "a high-tech lynching . . ." Anita Miller, ed., *The Complete Transcripts of the Clarence Thomas–Anita Hill Hearings: October 11, 12, 13, 1991* (Chicago: Chicago Review Press, 2005), p. 118.

p. 34: "the single most corrupt . . ." Alan M. Dershowitz, *Supreme Injustice: How the High Court Hijacked Election 2000* (New York: Oxford University Press, 2001), p. 174.

p. 37: "use all necessary and appropriate . . ." Public Law 107-40, 107th Congress. http://www.gpo.gov/fdsys/pkg/PLAW-107publ40/html/PLAW-107publ40.htm

p. 40: "We Republicans . . ." Jeffrey Toobin, "Blowing Up the Senate," *The New Yorker* (March 7, 2005). http://www.newyorker.com/magazine/2005/03/07/blowing-up-the-senate

p. 40: "One vote matters . . ." "Frist Campaigns Against Daschle in South Dakota," FoxNews.com, May 27, 2004. http://www.foxnews.com/story/2004/05/27/frist-campaigns-against-daschle-in-south-dakota.html

p. 40: "It used to be unheard of . . ." Ibid.

p. 40: "I feel like every morning . . ." Jonathan Weisman and Charles Babington, "Iraq War Debate Eclipses All Other Issues," *Washington Post*, November

20, 2005. http://www.washingtonpost.com/wp-dyn/content/article/2005/11/19/AR2005111901249.html

p. 43:   "You may call it . . ." David Herszenhorn, "How the Filibuster Became the Rule," *New York Times*, December 2, 2007. http://www.nytimes.com/2007/12/02/weekinreview/02herszenhorn.html?_r = 0

p. 44:   "I think we can stipulate . . ." Ibid.

p. 45:   "As the Republican Party has moved . . ." "Longtime GOP Sen. Arlen Specter Becomes Democrat," CNN, April 28, 2009. http://www.cnn.com/2009/POLITICS/04/28/specter.party.switch/

p. 50:   "to pass a partisan bill . . ." , Michael K. Gusmano, "Health Care Reform," in *The Obama Presidency: A Preliminary Assessment*, ed. by Robert P. Watson, et al. (Albany: State University of New York Press, 2012), p. 205.

p. 51:   "the culmination of a year-long . . ." WHAS staff, "Partisan Reaction to Healthcare Bill Passage," WHAS11.com. http://www.whas11.com/story/news/politics/2014/10/09/15319110/

p. 51:   "It was absolutely critical . . ." Alec MacGillis, *The Cynic: The Political Education of Mitch McConnell* (New York: Simon & Schuster, 2014), p. 108.

p. 52:   "We must address the issue . . ." Ibid., p. 107.

p. 52:   "Never before have cosponsors . . ." Thomas E. Mann and Norman J. Ornstein, *It's Even Worse Than It Looks: How the American Constitutional System Collided with the New Politics of Extremism* (New York: Basic Books, 2013), p. xx.

p. 53:   "This gridlock and dysfunction . . ." Carl Hulse, "Newly Empowered, Mitch McConnell Promises an End to 'Gridlock,'" *New York Times*, November 5, 2014. http://www.nytimes.com/2014/11/06/us/politics/victory-assured-gop-to-act-fast-in-promoting-agenda-in-congress.html?_r = 0

p. 55:   "It's kind of hard . . ." Ailsa Chang, "McConnell's Call for 'Regular Order' May Not Mean What It Used To," *Weekend Edition*, National Public Radio, February 8, 2015.

Glossary

bipartisan—referring to agreement or cooperation between two political parties that have opposing policies and ideological beliefs.

caucus—all the members of the Democratic or Republican Party in Congress, or a subset of them; a meeting of the members of a legislative body who are members of a particular political party, to select candidates or decide policy for that party.

cloture—in a legislative assembly, a procedure for ending a debate and taking a vote.

constituent—a voting member of a community.

filibuster—an action, such as a prolonged speech, that obstructs progress in a legislative assembly while not violating the assembly's procedures.

gridlock—a situation in which no progress or movement is possible.

incumbent—someone who already holds the office and is campaigning for reelection.

loophole—an ambiguity, often unintentional, in a law or a legal agreement, which allows an individual or corporation to get around the intent of the law, agreement, or regulation.

midterm election—in federal politics, the congressional election that is held two years after each presidential election.

partisan—a strong supporter of a party, cause, or person.

Further Reading

Adler, E. Scott, and John D. Wilkerson. *Congress and the Politics of Problem Solving*. New York: Cambridge University Press, 2013.

Bardes, Barbara, Mack Shelly, and Steffen Schmidt. *American Government and Politics Today: Essentials 2015-16 Edition*. Boston: Cengage Learning, 2015.

Handlin, Amy. *Dirty Deals? An Encyclopedia of Lobbying, Political Influence, and Corruption*. Santa Barbara, Calif.: ABC-CLIO, 2014.

Koger, Gregory. *Filibustering: A Political History of Obstruction in the House and Senate*. Chicago: University of Chicago Press, 2010.

La Raja, Raymond J. *Small Change: Money, Political Parties, and Campaign Finance Reform*. Ann Arbor: University of Michigan Press, 2008.

MacNeil, Neil, and Richard A. Baker. *The American Senate: An Insider's History*. New York: Oxford University Press, 2013.

Mann, Thomas E., and Norman J. Ornstein. *It's Even Worse Than It Looks: How the American Constitutional System Collided with the New Politics of Extremism*. New York: Basic Books, 2013.

Smith, Steven S. *The Senate Syndrome: The Evolution of Procedural Warfare in the Modern U.S. Senate*. Norman: University of Oklahoma Press, 2014.

Internet Resources

http://www.senate.gov
> The official website of the United States Senate.

http://www.senate.gov/legislative/votes.htm
> This page tracks roll-call votes in the Senate.

http://www.rollcall.com
> The online version of *Roll Call*, a Washington, D.C.–based newspaper focusing on politics and policy.

https://www.democrats.org
> Home page of the Democratic National Committee (DNC), an organization that provides leadership for the Democratic Party. The DNC coordinates national fundraising efforts and election strategy. It also develops and promotes the party platform—a list of its positions on various current issues.

https://www.gop.com
> The home page of the Republican National Committee, which provides leadership for the party. It includes articles about Republican candidates, as well as the Republican position on current issues, known as the party platform.

Index

Numbers in **bold italic** refer to captions.

liberals, 14, 26
> friendships of, with conservatives, 26–27
> and polarization measurement, 17–19, *20*, 21–22
> *See also* Democratic party

Mann, Thomas, 52
Mansfield, Mike, 23–24
Marshall, Thurgood, 30
McCain, John, *11*, 40
McConnell, Mitch, 9–10, 11, 44, 51–52, 53–55
Menendez, Robert, 7
Mikulski, Barbara, 32

National Journal, 17–19, 21
Nelson, Ben, 48
No Child Left Behind Act, 36
"nuclear option," 9–10, 11, 12

Obama, Barack, 8–9, 10, 11, 16, 19, 45, 46, *47*, 49, 50, 52, *54*, 55
O'Donnell, Christine, 16
Ornstein, Norman, 6, 52

"party unity" votes, 16–17
Patient Protection and Affordable Care Act. *See* Affordable Care Act
Paul, Rand, 16
Pelosi, Nancy, 49, *54*
polarization, Senate
> history of, 13–17, 21–22, 25–26
> measurement of, 17–19, *20*, 21–22
> *See also* Senate
Poole, Keith T., 21–22

Rangel, Charlie, 43
Reagan, Ronald, 13, 25, 29–30
reciprocity, 25
reconciliation, 49–51
Reid, Harry, 9, 10–11, 16, 41, 53, 54–55

Republican party, 11–12, 13–15, 18–19, *20*, 21–22, 33, 53
> and Bork nomination, 30
> and Conrad-Gregg proposal, 52
> and filibusters, 8–11, 40, 43, 48, 49, 52
> as majority party in Senate, 25, 35–36, 39–40, 53
> and role of government, 13, 14
> and the Tea Party movement, 15–16
> and Thomas nomination, 31–32
Rosenthal, Howard, 21–22
Rubio, Marco, 16

Schickler, Eric, 25, 26
Schneider, Bill, 17
Senate
> and ambassador appointments, 5–6, 7, 8, 12
> centrism in the, 13–15, 16
> and Clinton impeachment, 32–33
> cloture votes in the, 23–24, 39, 43, 44, 53, 55
> committees in the, *5*, 7, 30–32, 46, 48
> deliberative design of the, 22–23
> diversity in the, 26, 32
> and the election controversy (2000), 34–36
> and filibusters, 8–11, 23–24, 25, 39–40, 43, 48, 49, 52
> friendships in the, 26–27
> and health care reform, 45–51
> and judicial nominations, 8, 9, 10–11, 23, 29–32, 39–40
> and legislation, 27, 36, 38, 39, 45–46, 48–52, 54–55
> and norms of restraint, 25–27, 40, 52
> and the "nuclear option," 9–10, 11, 12
> and number of senators, *5*
> and "party unity" votes, 16–17
> and polarization measurement, 17–19, *20*, 21–22
> and presidential appointments, 8–12, 23, 29–30, 39–40
> procedural rules in the, 6–8, 9, 10–11, 22–25, 53–54
> and senators' net worth, *43*
> and September 11 terrorist attack, 37–39
> and Supreme Court nominations, 11, 29–32
> and voice votes, 7
> women in the, 26, 32
"Senate Procedure: Precedents and Practices," 25
Sinclair, Barbara, 17
Snowe, Olympia, 17, 45, 46, 48
Specter, Arlen, 14, 32, 45
Supreme Court, 11, 29–31, 34

Tea Party movement, 15–16
> See also Republican party
terrorism, 37–39
Thomas, Clarence, *29*, 30–32
Toomey, Pat, 16

unanimous consent, 6–7
U.S. Senate. *See* Senate
USA PATRIOT Act, 38

Wawro, Gregory J., 25, 26

About the Author

John Ziff is a write and editor. He lives near Philadelphia. His books for young adults include *The Bombing of Hiroshima* (Chelsea House, 2002), *The Causes of World War I* (OTTN Publishing, 2005), *Gun Laws* (Eldorado Ink, 2014), *The Korean War* (Mason Crest, 2015) and *Northeast: New Jersey, New York, Pennsylvania* (Mason Crest, 2015).